Children's book author **Cécile Jugla** knows that the best way to learn about and understand science is by observing and doing experiments ... which is why she wrote and designed the *There's Science in* series, full of exciting discoveries.

Creator of the Cité des Enfants, and former director of the Palais de la Découverte science museum in France, **Jack Guichard** loves to bring scientific principles to life, making them accessible to everyone.

Laurent Simon illustrates books for children (and grown-ups, too), and sometimes he also writes them. He particularly likes to illustrate science books, though.

First American Edition 2024
Kane Miller, A Division of EDC Publishing

Copyright © 2019 by Editions NATHAN, SEJER, Paris — France,
Édition orignale: *La science est dans l'œuf*

All rights reserved. No part of this publication may be reproduced, stored in a retrieval system, or transmitted, in any form or by any means (electronic, mechanical, photocopying, recording or otherwise), without the prior written permission of the publisher.

For information contact:
Kane Miller, A Division of EDC Publishing
5402 S 122nd E Ave, Tulsa, OK 74146
www.kanemiller.com
www.paperpie.com

Library of Congress Control Number: 2023938247
Printed and bound in France
1 2 3 4 5 6 7 8 9 10
ISBN: 978-1-68464-755-2

All photos © Shutterstock

Cluck! Cluck! I'm the one laying eggs!

Text by **Cécile Jugla** and **Jack Guichard**

Illustrations by Laurent Simon

A DIVISION OF EDC PUBLISHING

# Contents

8 GET TO KNOW YOUR EGG

10 WHAT'S INSIDE YOUR EGG?

12 TEST THE STRENGTH OF YOUR EGGS

14 LOOK FOR HOLES ON THE EGGSHELL

16 HOW OLD IS YOUR EGG?

- 18 COOK YOUR EGG
- 20 MAKE YOUR EGGS DANCE
- 22 MAKE YOUR EGGSHELL DISAPPEAR
- 24 GET YOUR EGG INTO A BOTTLE
- 26 MAKE MAYONNAISE
- 28 BEATING YOUR EGG WHITES

GET TO KNOW YOUR EGG

Do you have a chicken egg in front of you?
OK! Let's take a closer look.

What shape is it?

square   round   oval   triangle   hard to say

Answer: oval

What color is it?

beige   green with yellow spots   violet   black-and-white   white   dark brown

Answer: beige, white, or dark brown

Is it as heavy as:

a small container of yogurt?   a kiwi?   a bottle of water?

Answer: a kiwi

The color of eggs varies according to the breed of hens and what they eat: some eggs can even be greenish blue!

WHAT'S INSIDE YOUR EGG?

Crack your egg open on a plate.

It's fun to pull on the membrane!

When the air pocket is punctured, the air escapes.

Pfff!

Did you know?
Feeding crushed oyster shells to chickens makes their eggshells stronger.

Knock, knock! Who's there?

The shell membrane stops bacteria from entering the egg.

The chick grows from **the germinal disc**: you need to look closely to see it!

The chick absorbs **the yolk** first.

The chalaza is like a spring that holds the yolk in the center of the egg.

The yolk membrane separates the yolk from the white.

The white protects the chick from cold weather and shocks. The chick absorbs it after the yolk.

It's amazing: the egg has everything the chick needs to grow.

The air pocket is located at the large end of the egg.

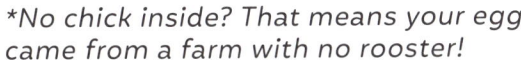
*No chick inside? That means your egg came from a farm with no rooster!

Well done! You've learned the anatomy of your egg!

TEST THE STRENGTH OF YOUR EGGS

I'm cutting the tops off the small cones in the center of the egg carton.

CLICK!

Why doesn't the eggshell break?

The eggshell is **light**: it weighs about the same as a sugar cube!

force

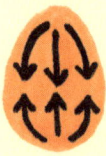

It is made of very small pieces of **limestone crystals** connected to each other. They form **arches** inside the shell ...

12

LOOK FOR HOLES ON THE EGGSHELL

"I can see lots of tiny holes with my magnifying glass."

"There are 10,000 of them. They are called pores."

"We say that the shell is porous."

The pores prevent large microbes from entering the egg ...

BANG!

... but not air. So if a chick is inside, it can breathe!

How can we be sure that air goes through the eggshell?

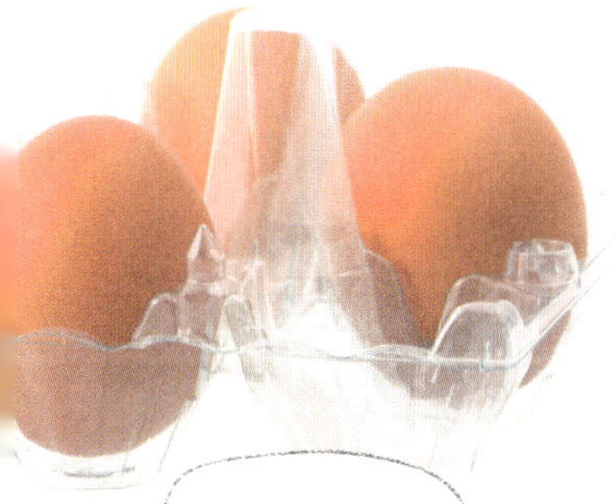

Take a raw egg...

...and use a spoon to add it to a glass of hot water.

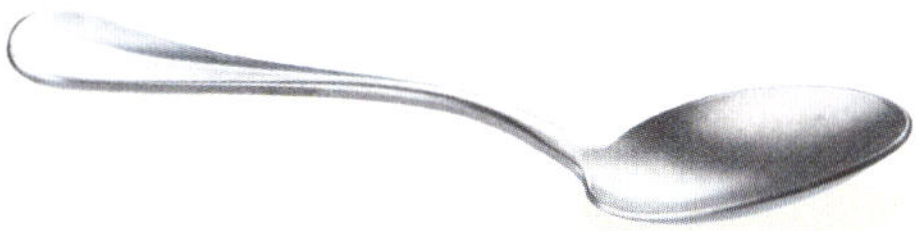

Oh! There are lots of bubbles around the large end of the egg!

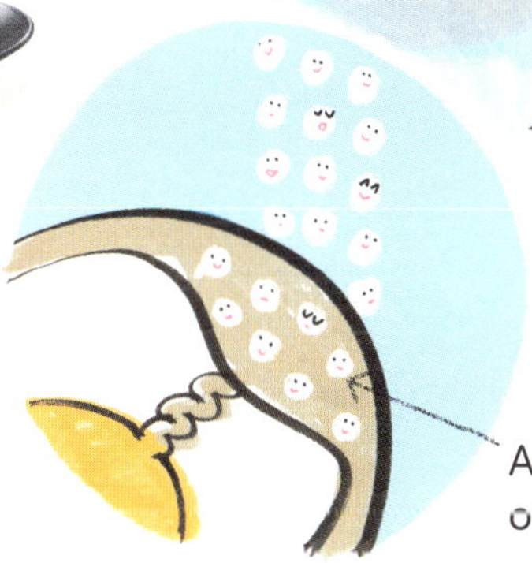

Air bubbles are coming out of the air pocket.

Why do bubbles come out of the air pocket?

Because of **the heat**! The **air in the air pocket** takes up **more space** when heated and so must escape through the pores in the shell.

You are a champion of experiments! You proved that an eggshell is porous!

HOW OLD IS YOUR EGG?

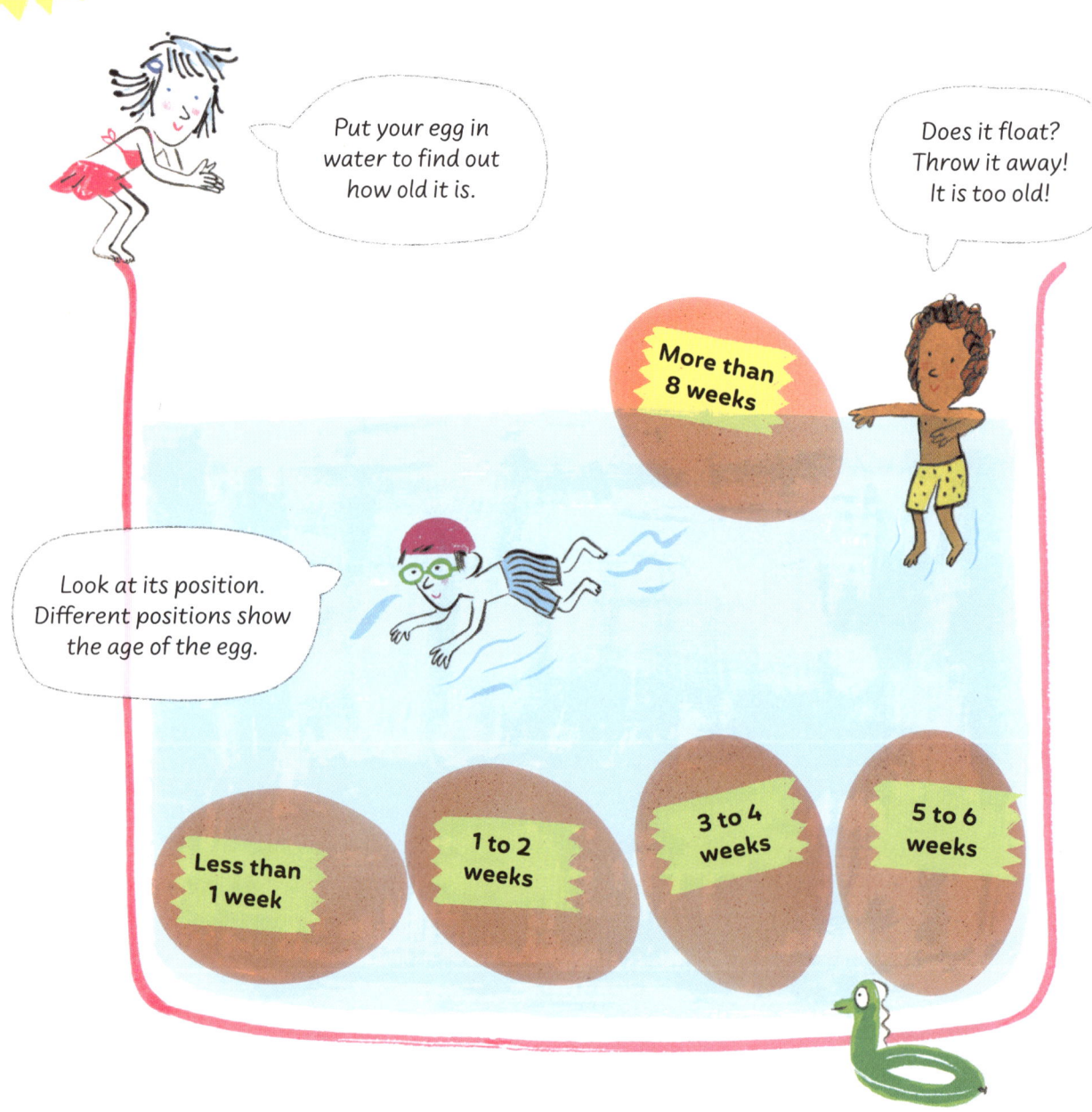

Why does an old egg float?

With time, the white loses water and the yolk releases gas. They take up less space so the air pocket grows.

The bigger the air pocket gets, the lighter the egg gets, so it can stand on end.

When the air pocket is very big, the egg becomes lighter than water, and it floats.

The science behind this is called Archimedes' principle: it explains why an old egg floats.

COOK YOUR EGG

I'm carefully dropping 3 eggs into a pot of boiling water.

I'm setting the timer.

3 minutes: soft-boiled egg
The yolk is runny and the white is mostly firm.

How do eggs cook?

We won!

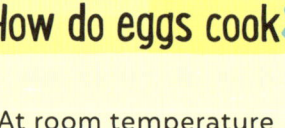

At room temperature, the egg white, made of a lot of water, is **liquid**. It also contains other microscopic elements, all tightly packed.

With heat, these elements unfold and form a net, which traps the water. The egg white becomes **solid** ... or firm.

5 minutes: medium-boiled egg
The yolk is jammy and the white is firm.

10 minutes: hard-boiled egg
Both the white and the yolk are firm.

In life, you don't need to hurry!

It is the **same for the yolk**, except it takes longer!

Congratulations! You've learned how heat changes an egg from a liquid to a solid.

MAKE YOUR EGGS DANCE

Use your fingertips to make a raw egg and a hard-boiled egg spin.

Ready, Set, Go!

I'm turning slowly!

And I'm turning very quickly!

On this side is **the raw egg**: its liquid egg white and yolk **slow it down**.

And here's **the hard-boiled egg**: its cooked egg white and yolk form a solid that **does not slow down** its momentum!

Don't use a tablecloth or place mat—the eggs won't easily spin.

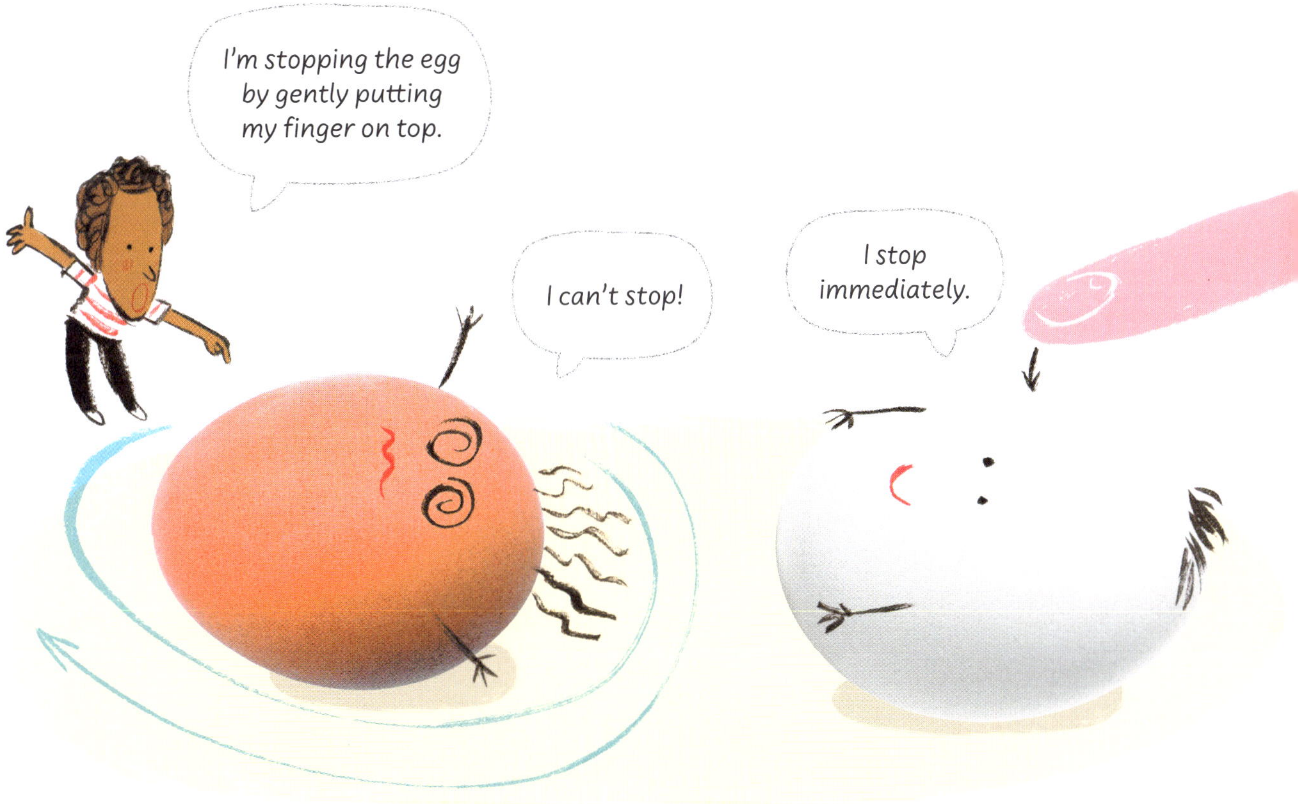

I'm stopping the egg by gently putting my finger on top.

I can't stop!

I stop immediately.

When you put your finger on the top of **the raw egg**, the liquids inside **keep turning** and that keeps **spinning** the egg: this is **the force of inertia**!

When you touch **the hard-boiled egg**, the yolk-white solid that fills the egg shell completely **stops** spinning.

Well done, you are the champion of spin! And you have discovered the law of inertia!

MAKE YOUR EGGSHELL DISAPPEAR

Put your egg in a glass.

Cover it with white vinegar.

Bubbles will appear around the shell.

We are bubbles of the gas carbon dioxide.

Why are there bubbles

The shell is made **of limestone**, like chalk. The acid of the vinegar **eats away** or **dissolves** the shell's limestone. The meeting between the two creates **a chemical reaction**: it produces **carbon dioxide** bubbles.

What does your egg look like 24 hours later?

The eggshell is gone! What remains is **soft** and the egg is **bigger**. It "drank" the vinegar.

Oh no! I'm naked!

Yikes!

The membrane surrounding it is strong and ... **elastic!**

Make your egg bounce!

Look at me! I'm bouncing!

Whoops!

Bleurgh!

Beware! Your egg will burst if it is thrown from a height of more than 8 inches.

Excellent chemistry! You have experimented with the principle of dissolving limestone with acid.

GET YOUR EGG INTO A BOTTLE

Put a peeled hard-boiled egg on an empty glass bottle.

Ask an adult to help you fill a bowl with very hot water.

The opening of the bottle should be a little bit smaller than the egg.

Oh, the egg is bouncing. It looks funny!

Why does the egg bounce?

With **heat**, **the air** in the bottle **expands**: its microscopic elements spread out and take up more space. They push the egg, which bounces in the air!

A little extra tip

To get the egg out, have an adult hold the bottle upside down under hot tap water.

Why does the egg fall?

When it cools, **the air** in the bottle **shrinks: its microscopic elements tighten and take up less space.** Thanks to its oval shape and its elasticity, the egg slides into the bottle.

Nice work! You just learned that air expands and contracts with heat and cold!

MAKE MAYONNAISE

Mix one egg yolk with a teaspoon of mustard, a little vinegar, and salt and pepper.

salt

pepper

vinegar

Save the egg white for the next experiment.

egg yolk

The egg should be at room temperature.

mustard

A little extra tip

How to easily separate the yolk from the white!

 Squeeze the air out of a small empty plastic bottle by pressing on it.

 Still pressing, put the top over the yolk. Gently release for the bottle to suck up the yolk.

 Place the bottle over a plate. Squeeze the bottle again, and the yolk falls.

What happens with water and oil ?

Usually when you mix water and oil, the oil rises quickly and floats above the water. It is **an unstable emulsion**.

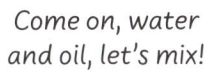

In mayonnaise, the microscopic elements of the egg yolk bring together the oil with the water from the yolk, and the mustard, and the vinegar. They create **a stable emulsion**.

Awesome! The principle of emulsion is no longer a mystery to you!

# BEATING THE EGG WHITES

Ask an adult to help you whip 3 or 4 egg whites. See how big they get!

How do egg whites change

When you start whipping, air bubbles enter the egg white. They take up space, and **it grows**!

So cool!

As you continue to whip, the air bubbles become smaller; the whites **harden,** trapping the bubbles.

"The egg whites have become white in color and firm, just like snowy mountain peaks!"

"They are so firm that the glass does not sink."

A little extra tip

Mix the whipped egg whites with 1/4 cup sugar and 1/4 tsp cream of tartar. Bake small spoonfuls of the mixture in a 425° oven. The water will evaporate, and the whites will harden to become meringues!

What a great scientist! You have tested the role of a surfactant to trap air bubbles.